SPAIN

SPAIN

The Kingdom of the Sun

Claudia Martin

Copyright © 2024 Amber Books Ltd

All rights reserved. No part of this publication may be reproduced, stored in a retrieval system, or transmitted in any form or by any means, electronic, mechanical, photocopying, recording, or otherwise, without prior written permission of the copyright holder.

Published by
Amber Books Ltd
United House
North Road
London N7 9DP
United Kingdom

www.amberbooks.co.uk
Facebook: amberbooks
YouTube: amberbooksltd
Instagram: amberbooksltd
X(Twitter): @amberbooks

ISBN 978-1-83886-430-9

Project Editor: Anna Brownbridge
Designer: Rick Fawcett
Picture Research: Adam Gnych

Printed in China

Contents

Introduction	6
Northern Spain	8
Central Spain	48
Eastern Spain	78
Southern Spain	118
The Islands: Balearics	174
The Islands: Canaries	202
Picture Credits	224

Introduction

The first signs of ancestral human habitation in Spain date back 1.3 million years. Since then, a succession of settlers – from the Iberians and Romans to the Umayyads and Romani – have left their linguistic and cultural stamps on Spain, making it the vibrant and astounding country it is today. Over the three millennia since Bronze Age builders first made their mark

on Menorca, Spain's architects and craftspeople have given us an astounding number of architectural masterpieces, which have never failed to push the boundaries of what seems possible, from the piggy-backing arches of Córdoba's Mezquita to the soaring spires of Gaudí's Sagrada Família. These jewels grace a landscape that astounds by the variety of its beauties, from the peaks of the Pyrenees to the wetlands and windswept dunes of the southwest.

ABOVE:
La Escalinata, Teruel, Aragon
Built in 1920, this grand staircase's ornamental brickwork and tiles echo the work of the Mudéjars, the Muslims who stayed in Spain after the Reconquista.

OPPOSITE:
Zubizuri, Bilbao, Basque Country
Spanish architect Santiago Calatrava designed this sculptural 1997 footbridge. Its curved walkway is supported by steel cables from a winglike overhead arch.

Northern Spain

This region is a swathe of granite peaks, windswept beaches and verdant valleys. Straddling the border with France are the glacier-capped Pyrenees, which stretch for 450km (280 miles) from the Mediterranean Sea to the Bay of Biscay. From there, the baton is taken up by the Cantabrian Mountains, which extend over 300km (180 miles) along the coast of the Cantabrian Sea to the Galician Massif. The Cantabrian Mountains form a divide between Spain's dry central plateau and España Verde ('Green Spain') to the north, as their northern slopes receive plentiful rain from the Atlantic, putting the southern slopes in rain shadow. Green Spain, known for its lush fields and forests of beech and oak, stretches from the autonomous community of Galicia in the west to the Basque Country in the east. This green region is home to two of Spain's co-official languages, Galician and Basque, as well as the protected language of Asturian. To the east, in the Pyrenees, visitors will meet speakers of two more co-official languages, Catalan and Aranese, plus the protected Aragonese. These languages are a reflection of the distinct histories, characters and arts of the regions to which they belong. Jewels in those regions' crowns range from the pre-Romanesque architectural masterpieces of Asturias to the exceptional cuisine of the Basque Country, which can be sampled in many a Michelin-starred restaurant or a *txikiteo* tapas crawl through the streets of Bilbao.

OPPOSITE:
Guggenheim Museum, Bilbao, Basque Country
Designed by Canadian-American architect Frank Gehry, this museum of modern art opened in 1997. Constructed on the bank of the Nervión River, the building's curving, interlocking forms have been likened to a ship readying to set sail. Yet the exterior's titanium panels catch the light like the scales of a writhing fish.

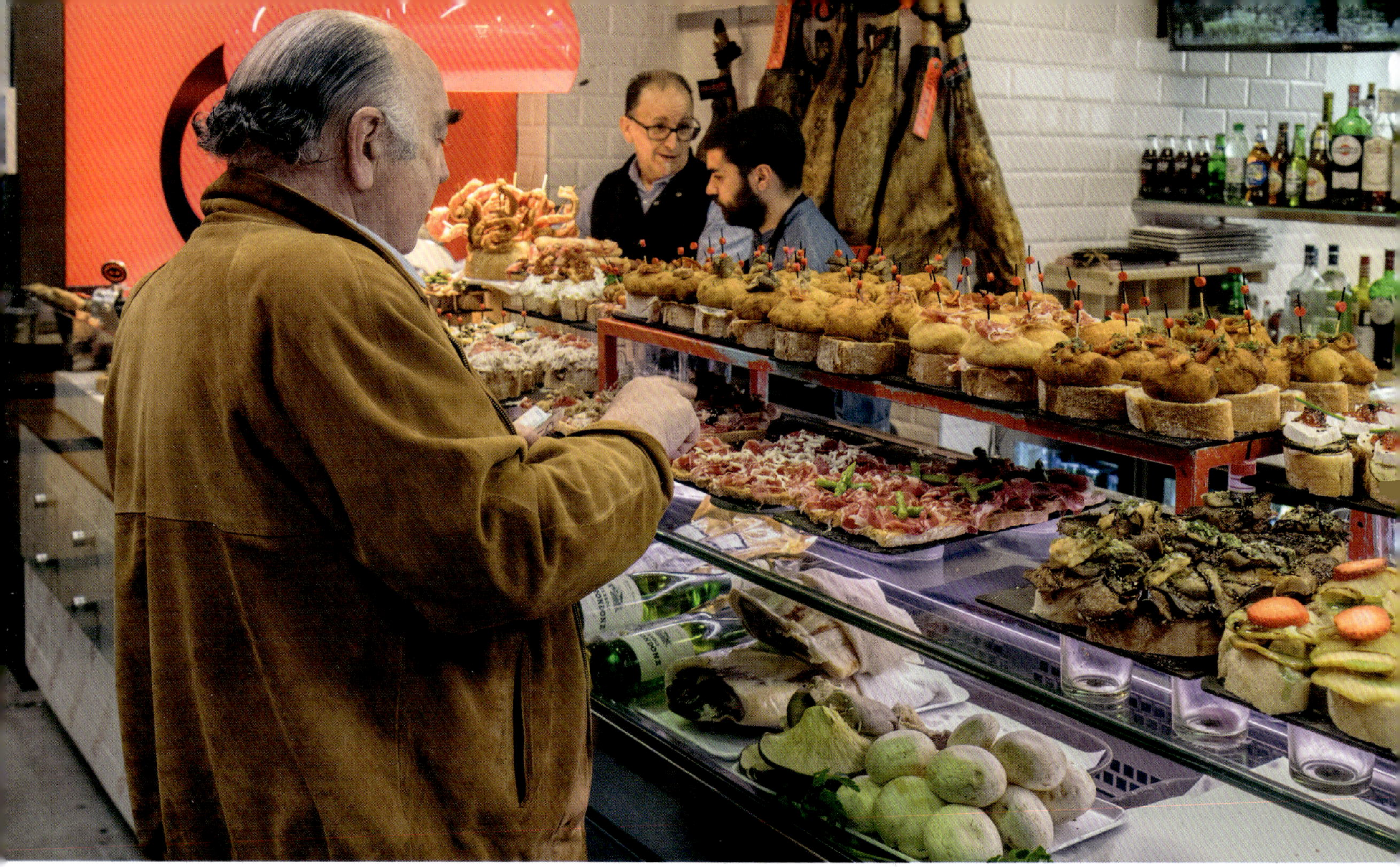

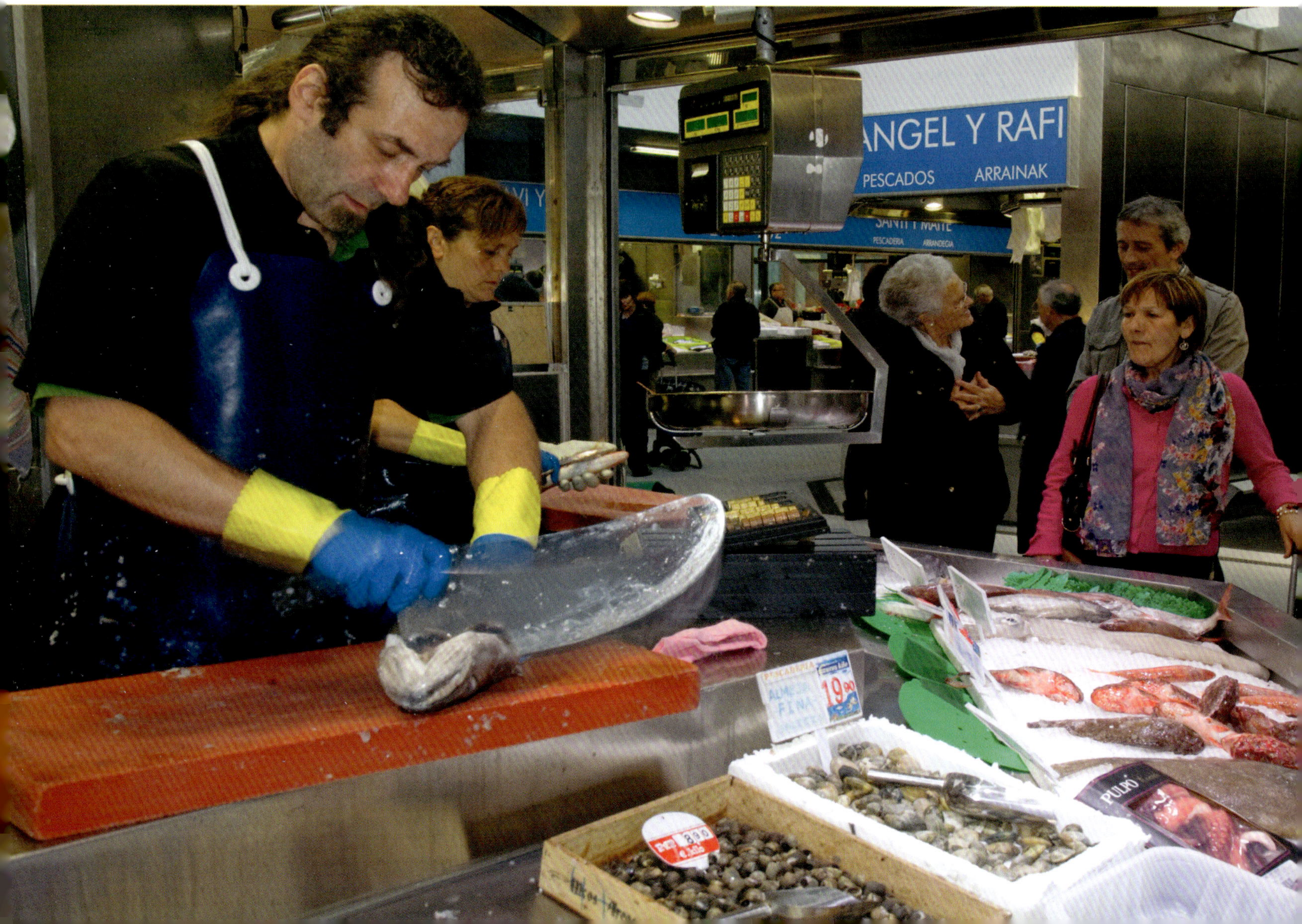
ANGEL Y RAFI
PESCADOS
ARRAINAK
PULPO

LEFT TOP AND BOTTOM:
Mercado de la Ribera, Bilbao, Basque Country
The biggest covered market in Europe, La Ribera covers 10,000 sq m (110,000 sq ft). More than 180 stalls offer fish, meat, fruit, vegetables, cheeses, mushrooms, local farmers' produce and *pintxos*. The stately, wedding cake-like Art Deco market building was designed in 1929 by Pedro Ispizua, who interned with the extraordinary Catalan architect Antoni Gaudí but went on to adopt a much more formal style.

ABOVE:
Plaza Nueva, Bilbao
Casa Victor Montes is known for its *pintxos*, traditional bar snacks consisting of ingredients secured to a slice of crusty bread with a toothpick. Specialities here include cheese-stuffed blinis, red scorpionfish cake and blood sausage with pine nuts. Victor Montes is one of many taverns and bar-restaurants that line the arcades of the Neoclassical Plaza Nueva, which is also home to the Euskaltzaindia, the Royal Academy of the Basque Language.

ABOVE AND RIGHT:
Aste Nagusia, Bilbao, Basque Country
The 'Great Week' festival is held over nine days from the first Saturday after 15 August, the Assumption of Mary. The festival's first event, known as the *txupinazo* in Basque, is the launch of a firework rocket from the balcony of the Arriaga opera house. This is presided over by the symbol of the festival, the giant Marijaia ('Mary festival') doll (pictured right), a woman with her arms raised in celebration. A favourite event with children is the Whale Parade, during which inflatable sea creatures process down the Gran Vía.

LEFT:
The *Sagrado Corazón* (Sacred Heart) statue, Castillo de la Mota, San Sebastián
Overlooking San Sebastián, on Mt Urgull, is a 12th-century castle, much rebuilt in the 16th century. Since 1950, the castle has been capped by a 12-m (39-ft) sculpture of Christ. The castle played a role in the 1813 Siege of San Sebastián, which ended in the burning of the town by British and Portuguese soldiers.

ABOVE:
Basílica de Santa María del Coro, San Sebastián, Basque Country
Located in this seafaring city's maze-like Parte Vieja ('Old Town'), the Basilica of St Mary of the Chorus was completed in 1774. The centrepiece of its Baroque facade is a statue of the tortured St Sebastian, who watches over the bustling shopping street of Calle Mayor.

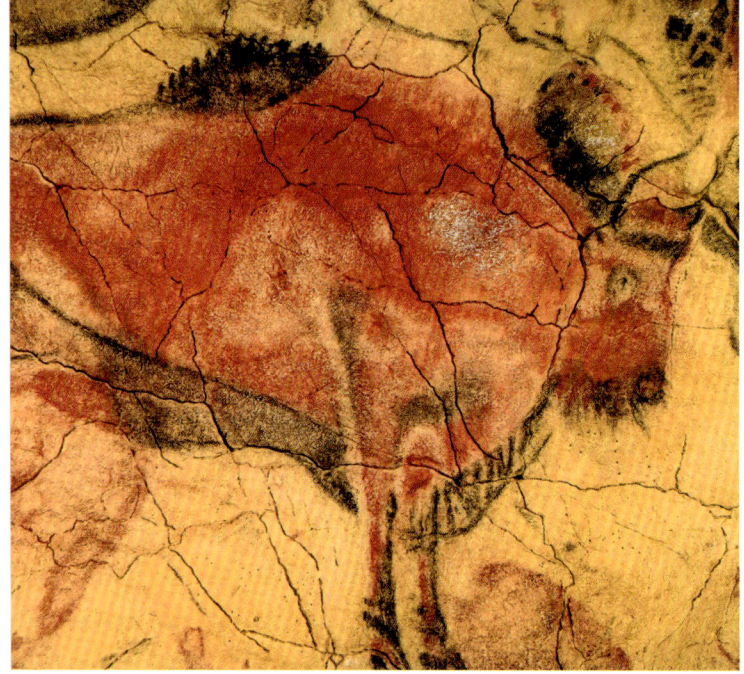

ALL PHOTOGRAPHS:
Cueva de Altamira, Cantabria
For more than 10,000 years, starting around 36,000 years ago, successive artists decorated the walls and ceilings of the Altamira cave complex with depictions of local fauna, including steppe bison and deer and outlines of their own hands. The artists used charcoal, ochre and haematite. Around 13,000 years ago, a rockfall sealed the cave's entrance, preserving its contents until rediscovery in 1868. Today, visitors can view the art only in a replica cave.

ABOVE AND LEFT:
El Capricho, Comillas, Cantabria
Antoní Gaudi designed only a handful of buildings outside Catalonia, including this exuberant orientalist villa in 1883–85. The tower, which resembles a Persian minaret, is capped with a playfully balanced canopy. The Moorish-style facade is jubilantly decorated with hundreds of tiles depicting sunflowers.

OPPOSITE:
Ruta del Cares, Picos de Europa National Park, Asturias
The largely guardrail-free Cares Gorge Trail stretches for 11km (7 miles) between the villages of Poncebos and Caín de Valdeón. Along the way, the trail hugs the vertiginous cliffside, crosses narrow bridges and ducks into tunnels before descending to the small green oasis of Caín.

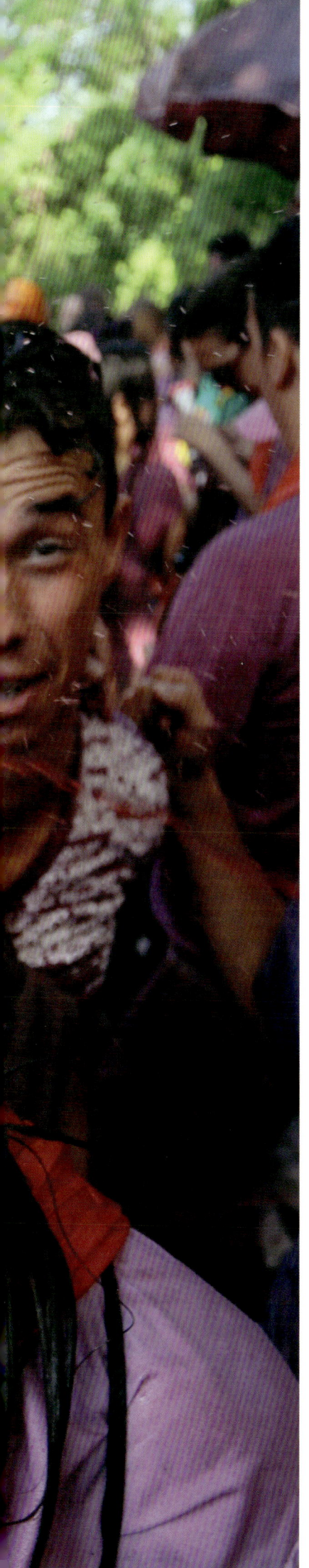

LEFT:
La Batalla del Vino, Haro, La Rioja
'The Wine Fight' takes place every year on 29 June in Haro, a town famed for its fine red wine. After early morning mass at the chapel of San Felices de Bilibio, the battle begins with participants dressed (initially) in white hurling wine at each other using bottles, water pistols and boots. Around 20,000 litres of wine are used.

ABOVE:
Wine Cellars, La Rioja
The hills of autonomous community La Rioja are cloaked by vineyards of red garnacha tinta, graciano, mazuelo and tempranillo grapes, as well as white garnacha blanca, malvasía and viura. The ageing of Rioja wines must be carried out in 225 litre (49.5 gal) oak barrels for six months to three years, then in the bottle for six months to six years.

Mazonovo, Taramundi, Asturias
The abandoned village of Mazonovo has been converted into a museum dedicated to the history of water mills, gravity mills and manual mills from around the world. The village was formerly the centre of flour production for its valley, which lies in the unspoiled Taramundi municipality, where farming is still the mainstay of the economy.

ABOVE:
Catedral de San Salvador, Oviedo, Asturias
With an 80m (262ft) Gothic tower, as well as pre-Romanesque, Romanesque and Baroque portions, this cathedral was founded in 781 CE but largely dates from the late 14th to mid-16th centuries. It is home to relics of St Eulogius and St Pelagius, both of whom were martyrs of Cordóba during the 9th and 10th centuries CE.

RIGHT:
San Julián de los Prados, Oviedo, Asturias
This masterpiece of pre-Romanesque Asturian architecture was built in around 830 CE when the Kingdom of Asturias was flourishing. The building was designed by Tioda, court architect to Alfonso II. Like other Asturian churches of the period, it has a basilical layout, is vaulted and exhibits Arabic influence in its rich internal decoration.

LEFT AND ABOVE:
Santa Cueva de Nuestra Señora de Covadonga, Covadonga, Asturias
This cliff-face sanctuary to Our Lady of Covadonga marks the entrance to a holy cave. It is said that Pelagius the Visigoth's forces retreated to the cave in around 718 CE during the Battle of Covadonga before defeating the army of the Umayyad Caliphate in the first successful skirmish of the Reconquista. In the cave, Pelagius prayed for help to a statue of the Virgin, which had been hidden there by a hermit. The current statue dates back to the 16th century.

Lagos de Covadonga, Asturias
Lake Ercina (pictured) and Lake Enol are a pair of shallow glacial lakes at a height of around 1130m (3720ft) in the Picos de Europa range. The steeply climbing road from Covadonga to the lakes is often part of the Vuelta a España multi-stage bicycle race.

PREVIOUS PAGE:
Catedral Basilica de Santiago de Compostela, Galicia
This magnificent cathedral is the reputed burial place of the apostle St James the Great, who is said to have brought Christianity to Iberia. The current cathedral was begun in 1075, with many later flourishes, and retains its stately Romanesque barrel-vaulted nave.

LEFT AND BELOW:
Camino de Santiago
The Way of St James has been a pilgrimage route since the 10th century CE. There are many starting points, one of the most common being Roncesvalles in the Spanish Pyrenees, from where it is 750km (465 miles) to the Basilica de Santiago de Compostela. The scallop shell (pictured on the route at Burgos) has long been the symbol of the Camino de Santiago, probably since medieval pilgrims started to take the shells as souvenirs from the beaches of Galicia.

LEFT:

Praia de Lumebó, Ferrol, Galicia
Known for its strong surf and dramatically sculpted rocks, this hard-to-reach beach can be quiet even on sunny summer days when a few nudists may relax on its soft, fine sand. The beach exists only at low tide when the west-facing cove offers a superlative vantage point for sunset-viewing.

OVERLEAF:

Encierro, Pamplona, Navarre
Pamplona's famous Running of the Bulls takes place in July during the festival of San Fermín. Six bulls and nine tame steers are released, taking around two minutes and 30 seconds to run at a speed of 24km/h (15mph) from their corral to the bullring 875m (2870ft) away. Human participants run only a short section of the course and then escape over the safety fence. However, since 1910, 15 people have been killed, most due to being gored.

Aigüestortes i Estany de Sant Maurici National Park, Catalonia
Catalonia's only national park lies in the Pyrenees, rising to 3023m (9918ft) at Besiberri Sud. Seasoned hikers take the Carros de Foc (Chariots of Fire) circular route (pictured), which connects nine of the park's mountain refuges. The luckiest walkers may spot some of the park's mammals, including brown bears, Pyrenean chamois and alpine marmots.

Cascada Gradas de Soaso, Ordesa y Monte Perdido National Park, Aragon
The hike to the Soaso Falls winds through the Ordesa Valley, where protected plants include Pyrenean narcissus, Pyrenean saxifrage and yellow gentian. The walk offers views of glacier-capped Monte Perdido to the northeast, the third-highest mountain in the Pyrenees, at 3355m (11,007ft).

Basílica de Nuestra Señora del Pilar, Zaragoza, Aragon
The small wooden statue of Our Lady of the Pillar (pictured far right) was probably carved by Juan de la Huerta in the mid-15th century. It stands on a tall pillar of jasper, which is draped in a skirt-like mantle. According to local tradition, in around 40 CE, Mary appeared to the apostle St James the Great on the banks of the Ebro River, gave him a column of jasper and instructed him to build a church in her honour.

Basílica de Nuestra Señora del Pilar, Zaragoza, Aragon
The current Cathedral-Basilica was built in Baroque style from 1681, with the most recent additions completed in 1961. The northwest tower can be climbed by lift and steps for views over the basilica's 11 tiled domes and the Ebro River.

ABOVE AND RIGHT:
Aljafería, Zaragoza, Aragon
This fortified palace was built in the 11th century by the Banu Hud dynasty, who ruled the Islamic Taifa of Zaragoza. In the palace's north wing, an arcade of multifoil arches is richly decorated with sinuous alfices (the moulding enclosing the arches' outer sides).

OPPOSITE:
Aínsa, Aragon
The village of Aínsa clusters around an 11th-century castle in the Huesca Pyrenees. Said to have been the capital of the semi-legendary medieval Kingdom of Sobrarbe, Aínsa is still a place of roughly hewn stone and cobbled streets. Restaurants serve local specialities such as *ternasco asado* (roast lamb) and *migas aragonesas* (fried bread topped with an egg).

Central Spain

Occupying the Meseta Central ('Central Tableland'), Spain's heartland is a semi-arid plateau bisected by the mountains of the Sistema Central. These ranges divide the drainage basin of the Douro, Iberia's highest-flow river, from that of the Tagus, the peninsula's longest river, which flows westwards from the plateau to the lower ground of Extremadura and then rushes to the Portuguese Coast. At the navel of the Meseta Central is Madrid, Europe's second-highest capital (after Andorra La Vella in the Pyrenees) at 650m (2130ft) above sea level. Although the site of the city was occupied in the Stone Age, the earliest documented settlement was in the second half of the 9th century CE when a citadel was built on the orders of Muhammad I, Umayyad emir of Córdoba. It was not until 1561, when Philip II moved the royal court to Madrid, that the city became the de facto capital of the Spanish Empire. Yet dynamic Madrid is only one of the great cities of the Meseta Central. To Madrid's southwest is Toledo, a capital of Visigothic Spain, the state that followed the fall of the Western Roman Empire. Today, Toledo is called the 'City of Three Cultures' due to the wildly creative influences of Christians, Muslims and Jews throughout its long history. To Madrid's northwest, in the autonomous community of Castile and León, three more history-rich cities form an isosceles triangle: Valladolid, Salamanca and Segovia, each vying for the crown of most beautiful townscape.

OPPOSITE:

Palacio Real, Madrid
The largest royal palace in Europe, this imposing Baroque mansion was built in the mid-18th century. Above its Grand Staircase is a 1759 fresco called *Spain Pays Homage to Religion and the Church* by Italian Rococo painter Corrado Giaquinto. It includes allegorical representations of Christianity, the Catholic Church, Truth, Strength, Vigilance, Reason and Counsel.

ABOVE TOP:
Gran Vía, Madrid
Madrid's Gran Vía is lined with masterpieces of revivalist architecture dating from the early 20th century. Buildings of note include the 1933 Rationalist Edificio Capitol (pictured left, topped with a Schweppes advert) and the 1925 brick-clad Palacio de la Prensa (pictured right).

ABOVE BOTTOM:
Palacio Real, Madrid
The Royal Palace's Grand Staircase was built in 1789 from San Augustin marble by Italian Neoclassical architect Francesco Sabatini, for whom the palace's Sabatini Gardens are named. On the landing are two lions carved by two different sculptors: Felipe de Castro and Robert Michel.

RIGHT:
Edificio Metrópolis, Madrid
On the corner of Gran Vía and Calle de Alcalá, the Metropolis Building was built in 1911 in Beaux-Arts style. Above the two-storey colonnade are four statues depicting Mining, Agriculture, Industry and Commerce. The cupola adorned with gold leaves is topped by a winged Victory.

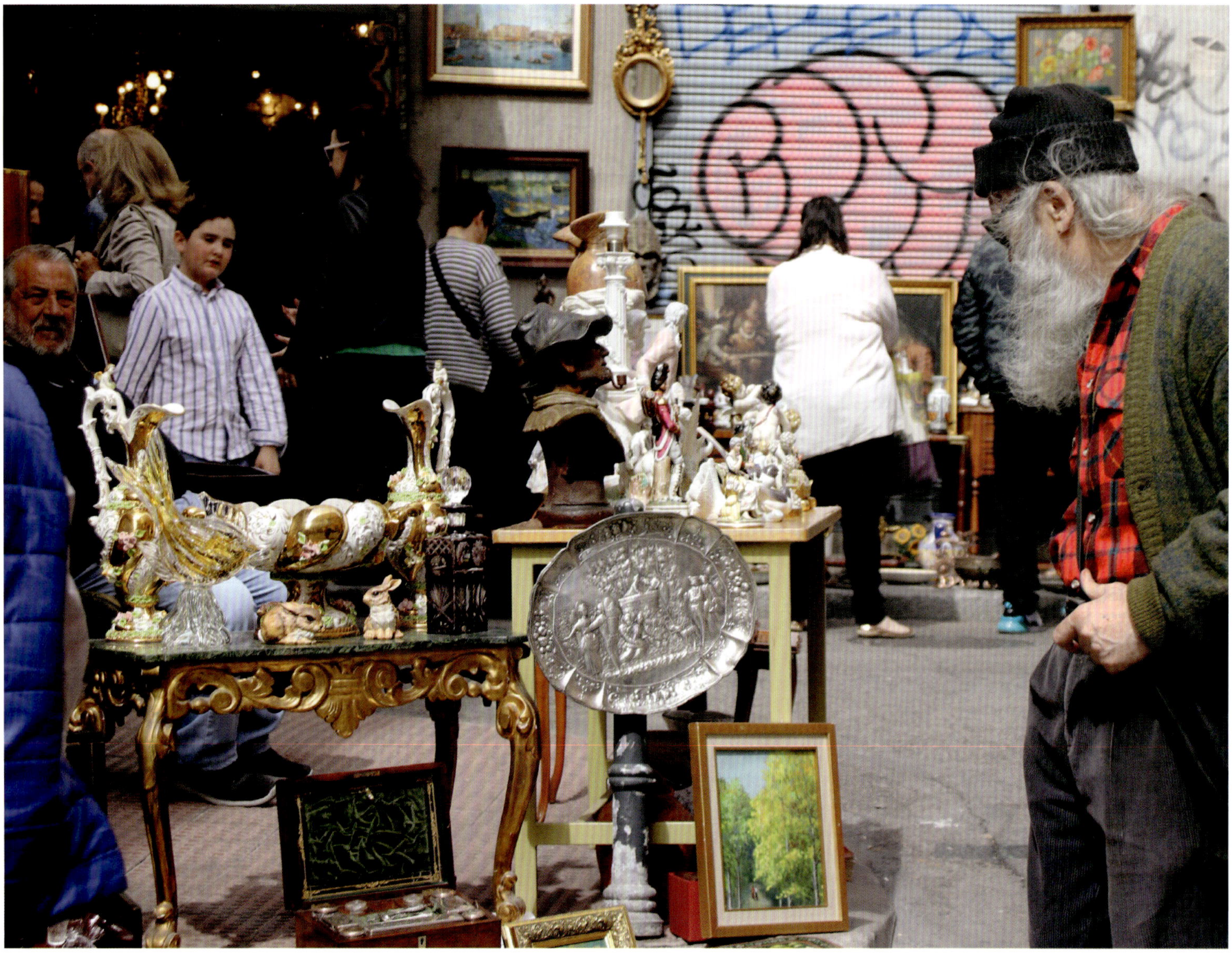

OPPOSITE TOP:
El Rastro, Embajadores, Madrid
This famous flea market takes place every Sunday in Embajadores, a neighbourhood known for its graffiti art and eclectic cuisine. The market offers bric-a-brac, from flamenco dresses and antiques to records and vintage dolls.

OPPOSITE BOTTOM AND ABOVE:
Malasaña, Madrid
In the 1980s, the Malasaña neighbourhood was the birthplace of the Movida Madrileña, a post-Franco countercultural movement bound up with punk rock, dada and vibrant street fashion. The movement rose alongside the use of Cheli, a jargon spoken only in Madrid. Today, Malasaña is still a centre of Madrid's dynamic nightlife scene.

LEFT:
Huertas, Madrid
Known officially as Barrio de las Letras ('The Literary Quarter'), this central neighbourhood takes its nickname from Calle Huertas, where the pavement is inscribed with quotes from Spanish authors, poets and philosophers. Miguel de Cervantes died nearby at Calle Cervantes 2. The neighbourhood is a choice stop for sampling Madrid-style tapas or buying the raw ingredients.

LEFT:
Estación de Atocha, Madrid
The old Atocha station had its tracks removed in 1992, then was repurposed as a tropical garden and complex of shops and restaurants. The wrought-iron structure was built in 1892 by Alberto de Palacio Elissagne with help from Gustave Eiffel.

ABOVE BOTTOM:
Templo de Debod, Madrid
Relocated due to the construction of the Aswan High Dam, this Egyptian temple to Amun was reconstructed in the Parque del Oeste in 1970–72. The temple was originally built in around 200 BCE in Nubia, close to the first cataract of the Nile.

ABOVE TOP:
Palacio de Cristal, Madrid
At the heart of Buen Retiro Park, the 'Glass Palace' is used for art exhibitions by the Reina Sofía Museum. Over 22m (72ft) high, the 1887 glass and iron building has a Greek-cross plan and is set on a brick base decorated with azulejo tilework.

El Escorial, San Lorenzo de El Escorial, Community of Madrid
The largest Renaissance building in the world, this monastery and royal palace complex was built between 1563 and 1584 for King Philip II. Since then, El Escorial's Royal Pantheon has been the burial place for most Spanish monarchs, up to Alfonso XIII (1886–1941).

ABOVE:
Aqueduct, Segovia, Castile and León
Built in the 1st century CE from unmortared granite blocks, this Roman aqueduct channelled water from the Acebeda River, 17km (11 miles) away, to Segovia until 1973. The aqueduct's elevated section over today's Plaza del Azoguejo has 167 arches.

FAR LEFT:
Walls of Ávila, Castile and León
Around 12m (39ft) high, Ávila's city walls were constructed between the 11th and 14th centuries. Around the walls' 2516m (8255ft) perimeter are 88 semicircular watchtowers and nine gates. Several city buildings are integrated into the fortification, including the apse of Ávila's cathedral.

LEFT:
Alcázar, Segovia, Castile and León
This crag at the western end of Segovia's old town was the site of a Roman castrum, an Almoravid fort and a Reconquista castle that evolved into a royal palace. However, much of what can be seen today – its towers and turrets allegedly inspiring Walt Disney – dates from an imaginative 1882 reconstruction following a devastating fire.

ABOVE TOP AND RIGHT:

Plaza Mayor, Valladolid, Castile and León
Valladolid's main square, designed by royal architect Francisco de Salamanca after a 1561 fire, became a model for other squares in Spain and the Americas, including Salamanca's Plaza Mayor. The square's immense space, lined with arcades and overlooked by balconies, was intended for use as a market and a stage for festivities.

ABOVE BOTTOM:

Plaza Mayor, Salamanca, Castile and León
Salamanca's harmonious main square was built from 1729 to 1755 by the Churriguera family of Baroque architects and sculptors. The spandrels of its arcaded sandstone buildings are adorned with medallions featuring the busts of notable figures, including kings and conquistadors. The square was used for bullfights until 1992.

ALL PHOTOGRAPHS:
Castillo de Zamora, Castile and León
Built in the 11th century with later additions, Zamora's castle was the linchpin of the city's fortifications during the Reconquista. The structure has a diamond-shaped plan and three towers, two of them pentagonal and the last heptagonal. The high walls are surrounded by a deep moat, which was once crossed by an unassailable drawbridge.

OPPOSITE:

Convento de San Esteban, Salamanca, Castile and León, This Dominican monastery was built over a lengthy period between 1524 and 1610. The extraordinarily ornate facade of the monastery's church is in Plateresque ('in the manner of a silversmith') style, which has roots in Mudéjar, Flamboyant Gothic and Lombard decoration.

ABOVE AND LEFT:

Casa de las Conchas, Salamanca Like the Convento de San Esteban, the 1493–1517 'House of Shells' has a Plateresque facade. The dominant element of its reliefs is more than 300 scallop shells, signalling that the owner, Rodrigo de Maldonado, was a knight of the Order of Santiago de Compostela. Members of the order used the scallop shell as a badge.

Alcázar, Toledo, Castilla–La Mancha
This fortified palace is on the site of an *al-qasr* built in the 10th century by Abd al-Rahman III, but was rebuilt first in the 16th century and then again after being damaged in the bloody 1936 Siege of the Alcázar during the Civil War. Each of the building's four 60-m (197-ft) towers has a Madrid-style spire, characterised by a pyramidal, dormered roof crowned with a lantern and topped with one or more metal spheres.

LEFT:
Puente de San Martín, Toledo, Castilla–La Mancha
Constructed in the late 14th century on the orders of Archbishop Pedro Tenorio, this bridge has five arches and fortified towers at both ends. The central arch spans 40m (130ft), a magnificent achievement for its medieval engineers.

ABOVE TOP:
Catedral Primada Santa María, Toledo
One of Spain's greatest High Gothic monuments, this cathedral was built between 1227 and 1493. Its spectacular tiled vaults are reinforced with cross-ribs known as liernes. The decorative ironwork screens, known as *rejas*, are 16th century.

ABOVE BOTTOM:
Sinagoga del Tránsito, Toledo
This synagogue was built around 1357 by Samuel HaLevi Abulafia, treasurer of King Pedro I of Castile. Today housing the Sephardi Museum, the synagogue became a church after the expulsion of the Jews from Spain in 1492. The Mudéjar-style prayer hall has characteristically detailed stucco work, multifoil arches and an *artesonado* ceiling, in which the interlaced rafters and laths form decorative geometric patterns.

Consuegra, Castilla–La Mancha
Twelve windmills, some dating to the 16th century, stand on a hill overlooking Consuegra. The windmills of this region first gained fame with the 1605 publication of Miguel de Cervantes' *Don Quixote*, which features a scene where the eponymous hero battles with windmills after mistaking them for giants.

ALL PHOTOGRAPHS:
Cuenca, Castilla–La Mancha
Located on a sheer-sided spur above the Huécar River, the town of Cuenca is known for its Casas Colgadas ('Hanging Houses'). With their wooden balconies jutting over the gorge, only a handful of these once-plentiful houses remain in the town, dating from the 15th century. In the town centre, the cathedral (pictured right) is one of the earliest examples of Gothic architecture in Spain. It was consecrated in 1196.

ALL PHOTOGRAPHS:
Monfragüe National Park, Extremadura
In the valley of the Tagus River, this national park hosts three main habitats: wetland, oak woodland and Mediterranean scrub. It is known for its birdlife, with 280 species counted among its visitors and year-round residents. Among these birds are 15 breeding species of raptors, including Eurasian griffon vultures (pictured above top). Among the park's water birds is the black stork (pictured above bottom), which feeds on fish, frogs and crabs.

76

ALL PHOTOGRAPHS:

Cáceres, Extremadura
Founded by the Romans in 25 BCE, Cáceres is a World Heritage City due to its melange of Roman, Moorish, Gothic, Renaissance and Baroque architecture. Remaining from the Islamic period are 30 towers along with a water cistern (pictured above) built between the 9th and 11th centuries CE. Among the city's more recent gems are the Gothic cathedral (pictured opposite bottom, on the skyline), the Baroque Church of San Francisco Javier (pictured opposite bottom, with two white towers) and the 15th-century Arco de la Estrella in the city wall (pictured left).

Eastern Spain

Stretching from the border with France to the ancient port of Cartagena in the southeast, this region encompasses five of Spain's 'Costas': Brava ('Wild'), Daurada ('Golden'), del Azahar ('Orange Blossom'), Blanca ('White') and Cálida ('Warm'). The Costas were named – or had their local names popularized – in the mid-20th century to promote stretches of Spain's 5755km (3575 mile) coastline to foreign tourists, yet the masterstroke of these marketing ploys was their truthfulness. Catalonia boasts two Costas: the northern, named for its rocky cliffs, and the southern, for its golden beaches. North of Valencia, in the region noted for its production of oranges, is the lesser-known 'Orange Blossom Coast'. Next is the 'White Coast', the moniker probably inspired by its long, white-sand beaches and whitewashed villages. Finally, the 'Warm Coast' occupies the shores of the Region of Murcia autonomous community, which is known for its subtropical semi-arid climate, giving it some of Spain's highest temperatures and lowest rainfall. Many of eastern Spain's allures lie on the narrow coastal plain, from Barcelona, the cradle of Catalan Modernisme, to Valencia, famed for its festivals and food. Yet, inland, in the Ebro Plain and in the mountains of the Iberian System, are lesser-known towns and villages with histories that were venerable long before the Romans stamped them on the map with forts and even longer before the Mudéjars graced them with exquisite craftsmanship.

OPPOSITE:

Sagrada Família, Barcelona, Catalonia
The largest incomplete Catholic Church in the world, the Sagrada Família was designed by Catalan Modernist architect Antoni Gaudí from 1883. When Gaudí died in 1926, less than a quarter of his part-Gothic, part-Art Nouveau, part-visionary structure was complete. The final decorative elements of the masterpiece may be complete by 2040.

ABOVE TOP:
Sagrada Família, Barcelona
Gaudí's design requires 18 spires, 13 of them built by 2023. The spires represent the Twelve Apostles, the Virgin Mary, the four Evangelists and Jesus Christ.

ABOVE BOTTOM:
Parc Güell, Barcelona
Designed by Gaudí from 1900, this Modernista park showcases traditional Catalan *trencadís* mosaics made of tile shards.

RIGHT:
Casa Milà, Barcelona
Eschewing structural rules, this undulating structure was the last private house built by Gaudí between 1906 and 1912. It is centred around two courtyards, which act as light wells. The building is nicknamed La Pedrera ('The Stone Quarry') due to its rough-hewn appearance, which belies the engineering excellence of its structural system of iron and brick pillars.

ABOVE AND RIGHT:
Casa Batlló, Barcelona
Nicknamed Casa dels Ossos ('House of Bones'), this Gaudí masterpiece was a 1904 remodel of an existing house. Moving far beyond Modernisme or Art Nouveau, the exterior of the organic, flowing structure resembles a writhing dragon, while the interior has vaulted, snail-like ceilings.

OPPOSITE
Casa Vicens, Barcelona
Built between 1883 and 1885, this house was one of Gaudí's first major works. Its checkerboard ceramic tiles, multilobed Nasrid arches and minaret-like towers are a playful take on the Orientalist and Neo-Mudéjar styles. The curling wrought-iron balconies supply contrast with the geometricity of the rest.

ABOVE AND OPPOSITE TOP:
La Boqueria, Barcelona
Entered from La Rambla, La Boqueria is always packed and noisy – even more so at lunchtime. Stalls sell meat, fish, olives, cheeses and pastries. A market has been held on this site since the 13th century.

RIGHT:
Tapas, Barcelona
Staples of Barcelonian tapas include *la bomba* (potato croquette stuffed with beef and topped with sauce), bread-based *pintxos*, *buñuelos de bacalao* (salt cod fritters) and the ubiquitous *pa amb tomàquet* ('bread with tomato').

OPPOSITE BOTTOM:
La Rambla, Barcelona
This pedestrianized 1.2km (0.75 mile) street has the landmark-rich Barri Gòtic ('Gothic Quarter') to its east and the edgier El Raval (from the Arabic for 'district') to its west.

ALL PHOTOGRAPHS:
Costa Brava, Catalonia
The shoreline of the province of Girona is known as the 'Wild Coast' due to its rugged cliffs and rocky coves, which are backed by forests of pine and cork oaks. Among the larger resorts is Tossa de Mar (pictured above), overlooked by a 12th-century castle. Quieter villages in which to eat seafood and swim in the turquoise sea include Cala Sa Tuna and Tamariu, named for its tamarisk trees.

ALL PHOTOGRAPHS:
Cadaqués, Catalonia
On the Costa Brava's Cap de Creus, the whitewashed fishing port of Cadaqués was beloved by artists including Pablo Picasso, Joan Miró, Marcel Duchamp and Salvador Dalí, who had a house nearby that is now a museum. The name Cadaqués probably comes from the Catalan *càdec*, meaning 'juniper', which grows abundantly here.

Teatre-Museu Dalí, Figueres, Catalonia
In the Surrealist artist's home town, the Dalí Theatre-Museum houses a vast and varied collection of his works, including the amusing *Mae West Lips Sofa*. The *Central Panel of the Wind Palace Ceiling* (pictured), completed in situ in 1972–3, includes portraits of Dalí and his wife Gala at the centre of a forced-perspective dream.

ALL PHOTOGRAPHS:
Besalú, Catalonia
This town's name has its roots in the Latin Bisuldunum, which means a fort on a mountain between two rivers. Besalú's jewel is its 12th-century Romanesque bridge, which has seven unequal arches and two fortified towers. Sections of the town's medieval walls still guard the narrow streets of the old town, where shops sell handicrafts made of willow, wood, iron and ceramics.

ALL PHOTOGRAPHS:
Girona, Catalonia
Girona's Romanesque baths (pictured opposite) were first documented in the 12th century but rebuilt by architect Ramon Taialà in 1294. The apodyterium (changing room), centred on an octagonal pool, was used as the 'Baths of Braavos' in the blockbuster television series *Game of Thrones*. Other locations for the series include the Sant Domenèc Stairs (above) and the cathedral (left), which was the 'Great Sept of Baelor' in season six. In reality, the cathedral was begun in the 11th century in Romanesque style, continued in Gothic style in the 13th century, and then given a Baroque facade in the 17th century.

PREVIOUS PAGE:
Cases de l'Onyar, Girona, Catalonia
Colourful houses overlook Girona's River Onyar where it is crossed by the pedestrian Pont d'en Gomez. The houses are painted according to a colour palette created by a team of Catalan artists and architects, including Fuses-Viader.

LEFT:
Sitges Carnival, Catalonia
A centre of Spain's LGBTQ+ culture, Sitges is famed for its Carnival, held during February and March, which attracts more than 300,000 people annually. Key events are the Rua de la Disbauxa ('Debauchery Parade') and Rua de l'Extermini ('Extermination Parade') on the night of Shrove Tuesday.

ALL PHOTOGRAPHS:

Casa Navàs, Reus, Catalonia
Built between 1901 and 1908, this residence was designed by Catalan Modernist architect Lluís Domènech i Montaner. In common with his other works, the building exhibits a balance between the curvilinear forms of Art Nouveau, the wonderful ornamentation of Spanish-Arabic architecture and the blockier structures of Rationalism.

ALL PHOTOGRAPHS:
Peixateria, Cambrils, Catalonia
With two Michelin-starred restaurants, many consider the fishing port of Cambrils to be the gastronomic capital of the Costa Daurada. The key ingredients in the local cuisine are, unsurprisingly, fish and seafood. Every weekday at around 5 p.m., the fishing boats unload their catch, including common dentex, Atlantic bonito, amberjack, bluefish and donax clams.

ALL PHOTOGRAPHS:
Tarragona, Catalonia
In around 218 BCE, the first Roman settlement on the Iberian Peninsula was Tarraco, today known as Tarragona. Around 200 years later, the Roman town was supplied with water by an aqueduct (pictured above), now called the Aqüeducte de les Ferreres, which stretched 15km (9 miles) from the Francolí River. Tarraco also had an amphitheatre (pictured left) built at the start of the 2nd century CE that seated up to 15,000 spectators.

LEFT:
Iglesia de San Pedro, Teruel, Aragon
This 14th-century church is a fine example of Aragonese Mudéjar architecture. The style is named for the Mudéjars, the Muslims who remained in Iberia after the Christian Reconquista and helped to introduce Islamic-style decorative elements into the Christian kingdoms. The church's interior was decorated between 1896 and 1902 in Neomudéjar Modernist style.

ABOVE:
Iglesia de San Salvador, Teruel
Built in the early 14th century, this Mudéjar belltower exhibits key features of the style, with its brick construction and elaborate geometric ornamentation giving it a close resemblance to an Almohad minaret. The bell chamber at the top of the 40m (130ft) tower offers spectacular views over Teruel through its elegantly arched windows.

Teatro Romano, Sagunto, Valencian Community
Sagunto's semicircular Roman theatre was built in the mid-1st century CE, when Roman Saguntum had around 50,000 inhabitants. Making use of the natural slope provided by a hill, the theatre had seats for around 8000 spectators. In addition to the theatre, which was for theatrical performances, the town had a circus for chariot racing.

109

OPPOSITE AND ABOVE:
Castell de Santa Bàrbara, Alicante, Valencian Community
Perched on the craggy summit of Mt Benacantil, this castle was first built as an Umayyad fort in the 9th century CE. It was captured by Castilian forces led by Alfonso of Castile in 1248, then rebuilt and expanded. In the 19th and 20th centuries, it was used as a prison and Francoist concentration camp.

LEFT:
Altea, Valencian Community
Although much of its income derives from tourism, Altea still has an unspoilt and photogenic old town, a maze of winding, whitewashed streets. In August, the town hosts the festival of Castell de l'Olla, when 50,000 spectators gather to watch spectacular fireworks launched over the water.

LEFT:

La Tomatina, Buñol, Valencian Community
Buñol's tomato-throwing festival has been held on the last Wednesday of August since 1945, when a fight spontaneously broke out involving produce unwillingly supplied by a market stall. Today, around 145,000kg (320,000 lb) of tomatoes are thrown by 20,000 ticket holders.

ABOVE TOP:

La Cremà, Fallas de Valencia, Valencian Community
The Fallas Festival is held in Valencia from 15–19 March in honour of St Joseph. On the last night, puppet-like figures known as *falles* (from the Valencian for 'torches') are burned in an event known as La Cremà ('The Burning'), followed by music and dancing long into the night.

ABOVE BOTTOM:

Falleras, Fallas de Valencia
Reines Falleras ('Queens of the Fallas Festival') process through the streets of Valencia during L'Ofrena de Flors ('The Flower Offering') on 17–18 March. Each Fallera carries flowers to be laid by a statue of the Virgin Mary. The beautiful traditional dresses worn by participants can cost as much as 20,000 euros.

LEFT:

Paella, Valencia, Valencian Community
Paella has its roots in the Valencia region, where rice was first grown – courtesy of the Umayyads – in the 10th century. 'Paella' is the Valencian word for frying pan. Traditional Valencian paella consists of *senia* rice, green beans, rabbit or chicken and *garrofó* beans, cooked in olive oil, chicken broth, rosemary and saffron.

ABOVE:

Falles, Fallas de Valencia, Valencian Community
At the heart of the Fallas Festival are the *falles*, which are complex assemblies of handmade dolls, each known as a *ninot*. The *falles* may be satirical, topical or fanciful. They are stuffed with fireworks and made of flammable materials so they can be burned (see p. 113).

LEFT:
Roman Theatre, Cartagena, Region of Murcia
Used for theatrical performances, this Roman theatre was built between 5 and 1 BCE. It had room for an audience of 6000 people. The wealthy Roman city of Carthago Nova ('New Carthage') was known for its silver mines and the production of the fermented fish sauce known as *garum*.

ABOVE TOP AND BOTTOM:
Lonja de la Seda, Valencia, Valencian Community
The Silk Exchange was built between 1482 and 1533 in Valencian Gothic style, which was popular in the region at the tail end of the broader Gothic period. The building was used for all kinds of commercial business, including the silk trade, which was the backbone of the port city's prosperity.

Southern Spain

Spain's southernmost mainland autonomous community is Andalucía. This region takes its name from the Arabic Al-Andalus, which possibly meant 'Land of the Vandals', referring to the Germanic people who had occupied Iberia in the 5th century CE. North Africans used the term Al-Andalus to mean the whole portion of the Iberian Peninsula ruled by Muslims for some or all of the years between 711 CE and 1492, but the name has stuck with only this southern region. This is apt, since it was here that the headline events of the Muslim conquest and Christian reconquest of Spain played out. It was in early 711 CE that commander Tariq ibn Ziyād sailed across the Straits of Gibraltar and began to wrest Spain from the Visigoths, gaining quick victory in the Battle of Guadalete, fought somewhere near Andalucía's Medina-Sidonia. It was on 2 January 1492 that Emir Muhammad XII surrendered the Emirate of Granada, the last Muslim territory in Spain, to Isabella I of Castile in the final act of the Reconquista. It was also in Andalucía that Muslim rulers, architects and craftspeople left their strongest marks, visible today in Granada's stunning Alhambra and Córdoba's Mezquita. Yet this region's architecture, art, music, dance and food also bear witness to the creativity and determination of settlers from places other than North Africa, including the Iberians, Phoenicians, Carthaginians, Romans, Vandals, Visigoths, Jews, Romanis and Castilians.

OPPOSITE:
Bodega, Jerez de la Frontera, Andalucía
Jerez gives its name to sherry, the fortified wine made in a triangular region of the province of Cádiz between Jerez de la Frontera, Sanlúcar de Barrameda and El Puerto de Santa María. Sherry is produced in styles ranging from the light fino to the dark and nutty oloroso, which oxidizes as it ages in the cask for at least two years.

OPPOSITE:
González Byass Bodega, Jerez de la Frontera, Andalucía
Fino sherry is aged in casks made of North American oak, which are filled five-sixths full to leave space for flor, a film of yeast, to develop on the wine. Flor gives fino sherry its distinctive bready taste. Old casks from this bodega are used by Scotch whisky producers to give their premium malts greater flavour.

LEFT:
Vineyard, Jerez de la Frontera
Three varieties of white grapes are grown for producing sherry: palomino, moscatel and Pedro Ximénez. Grapes are harvested in September. Palomino grapes, which make dry or light sherry, are pressed immediately, but moscatel and Pedro Ximénez grapes, which make sweet or darker wine, are left to dry and sweeten in the sun for two days.

ABOVE:
Feria del Caballo, Jerez de la Frontera
Jerez's 'Horse Fair' is held in the second week of May. The celebration has its roots in a medieval horse and cattle fair where deals were done and then sealed with a drink. Today, the fair offers horseriding and carriage displays, while the town's streets are lined with *casetas* serving fino sherry.

ALL PHOTOGRAPHS:
Parque Minero
Rio Tinto, Andalucía
The Rio Tinto Mining Park lets visitors access a dramatic human-made landscape that has been mined for almost 5000 years for copper, silver, gold and other minerals. The Rio Tinto gets its name (meaning 'red') thanks to very high levels of iron and metal sulfides dissolved in its highly acidic water. Little lives in the river except for lithoautotrophic bacteria that use sulfides as food.

BOTH PHOTOGRAPHS:

Greater Flamingos, Doñana National Park, Andalucía
Doñana National Park protects a wetland region in the delta where the Guadalquivir River meets the Atlantic Ocean. The park is known for its endangered species, such as the Iberian lynx, and more than 300 species of birds, including Spanish imperial eagles and greater flamingos. The largest species of flamingo, the greater, can reach 187cm (74in) tall. Like other flamingos, it gets its pink colouration from pigments known as carotenoids in its diet of brine shrimp and algae.

OPPOSITE:
Playa de Santa María, Cádiz, Andalucía
Occupying a small peninsula reached by a narrow isthmus, Cádiz has plenty of beaches. Playa de Santa María gives enticing views of the old town. On the western flank of the new town, Playa de la Victoria is often ranked as one of Spain's finest urban beaches, its sands stretching for 3km (1.9 miles).

LEFT AND BELOW:
Old Town, Cádiz
Founded by the Phoenicians perhaps as early as 1100 BCE, Cádiz is certainly one of western Europe's oldest continuously inhabited cities. Its crowded old town boasts a huge 1st-century BCE Roman theatre only discovered in 1980. The cathedral was built between 1722 and 1838, its lengthy construction endowing it with a Baroque facade (pictured below), Rococo trimmings and Neoclassical towers. It is crowned by a golden-tiled dome that glows in evening sunlight.

Carnaval de Cádiz, Andalucía
The Cádiz Carnival is famed for its groups of satirical singers known as *chirigotas*. These performers sing witty or serious songs about topical issues and events. Different musical forms can be used, including the pasodoble, a long and emotional song without a refrain, and the potpourri, which changes the lyrics of the year's popular songs.

ALL PHOTOGRAPHS:
Casa de Pilatos, Seville, Andalucía
Home of the Dukes of Medinaceli, this mainly 16th-century palace gained its name by becoming linked in the popular imagination with the house of Pontius Pilate after one of the palace's owners inaugurated the observance of the Holy Way of the Cross in Seville. The building is in Renaissance style, with the addition of hundreds of azulejo tiles. The statue of Athena in the main courtyard is believed to be from the Roman city of Italica, northwest of Seville.

Flamenco, Plaza de España, Seville, Andalucía
The flamenco style of music and dance had developed by the late 18th century within Andalucía's *gitano* community, which – like other Romani cultures – has its roots in the Indian subcontinent. Flamenco dance is characterized by strong emotion and stance, expressive arm movements and rhythmic foot stamps.

LEFT:
Baños de Doña María de Padilla, Real Alcázar, Seville, Andalucía
The Baths of María de Padilla is actually a Gothic vaulted water cistern beneath the Alcázar's Patio del Crucero. The cistern is named after a 14th-century mistress of Pedro I, despite being unrelated to her, as it was built in the 13th century during the reign of Alfonso X. The cistern was used as a location in season five of *Game of Thrones*.

ABOVE:
Plaza de España, Seville
This semicircular plaza and its pavilions were built for a 1929 world's fair: the Ibero-American Exposition. The flamboyant ensemble was designed by architect Aníbal González in a mixture of fashionable Art Deco style with Renaissance Revival elements and Neo-Mudéjar craftsmanship, seen particularly in the choice of brick and tile for its ornamentation.

ABOVE:

Santa Cruz, Seville, Andalucía
The former Jewish quarter is at the heart of old Seville. After the 1492 Alhambra Decree ordered the expulsion of Jews from Spain, the neighbourhood became a slum. In the 18th century, it was cleaned up, and its main synagogue was converted into a church. Today, the quarter's shady streets and squares are home to restaurants and bars.

RIGHT:

Real Alcázar, Seville
The Royal Palace began life as an Umayyad citadel in the early 10th century, then grew into an Almohad palace. After the Castilian conquest of 1248, it was rebuilt in Gothic, Renaissance and Mudéjar styles. In the 17th century, the Umayyad wall was transformed into a loggia (pictured) from which to enjoy the gardens.

ABOVE:
Churrero, Andalucía
A churros-maker uses hot oil to fry a wheel of pastry dough extruded from a star-shaped nozzle. Often eaten for breakfast, lengths of churro are usually sprinkled in sugar and then dipped in thick hot chocolate or coffee.

RIGHT:
Setas de Sevilla, Seville, Andalucía
Designed by German architect Jürgen Mayer, this immense wooden parasol was nicknamed the 'Mushrooms of Seville' when completed in 2011. It houses and shelters a museum, a marketplace, a viewing terrace and restaurants.

Playa de Bolonia, Costa de la Luz, Andalucía
Andalucía's Atlantic Coast is known aptly as the 'Coast of Light'. This stretch of shoreline has some of Spain's quietest, most undeveloped and most beautiful beaches, where – outside the summer months – visitors might meet only a few friendly dog walkers.

LEFT:
Estepona, Andalucía
On the Costa del Sol, midway between Gibraltar and Marbella is the pretty haven of Estepona, famed for its microclimate that provides more than 300 days of sunshine per year. Each street in the whitewashed old town has its own colour scheme of plant pots, from turquoise to lilac and coral.

ABOVE:
Tarifa, Andalucía
The town of Tarifa is located on the Punta de Tarifa, the southernmost point of continental Europe. It is one of the world's most popular destinations for wind sports, such as windsurfing and kitesurfing, due to the wind funnel of the Strait of Gibraltar.

OPPOSITE:

Alcazaba, Málaga, Andalucía
This fortified palace was built by the Hammudid dynasty in the early 11th century but was much altered by the Nasrids in the early 14th century. Constructed on a hilltop, the Alcazaba consists of two walled enclosures, one inside the other and additionally protected by towers. The inner enclosure contains the palaces.

ABOVE AND LEFT:

Catedral Basílica de la Encarnación, Málaga
Málaga's cathedral was constructed from 1528 to 1782 to the designs of Spanish Renaissance architect Diego de Siloe. The facade was embellished with Baroque flourishes long after Siloe's death. The cathedral was famously never finished due to lack of funds, with only one of its two towers completed: the single north tower is 84m (276ft) high.

Coro, Catedral Basílica de la Encarnación, Málaga
The choir of Málaga cathedral is home to two exquisite Baroque organs installed in 1782 at a cost of 60,000 ducats – a small fortune at the time. The elaborate 17th-century choir stalls sculpted from cedar and mahogany feature imaginative carvings of saints, plants, animals and round-cheeked cherubs.

ALL PHOTOGRAPHS:
Mercado Central de Atarazanas Málaga, Andalucía
Málaga's central food market is held in a late 19th-century iron and glass building that incorporates a monumental Nasrid gateway from the shipyard that once stood on the site. The building's stained-glass window features Málaga's architectural highlights.

BOTH PHOTOGRAPHS:
Frigiliana, Andalucía
Sited on a mountain ridge with spectacular views of the sea, Frigiliana has a picture-perfect old town of whitewashed houses and steep cobbled streets. In August, the town holds the 'Three Cultures Festival' to celebrate the creative confluence of Christian, Jewish and Muslim cultures in Frigiliana.

ABOVE:
Plaza del Socorro, Ronda, Andalucía
At a strategic height of 739m (2425ft) in the Sierra de las Nieves, Ronda was settled in the 6th century BCE. It has since been an important outpost for the Romans, Visigoths and Umayyads. In the 20th century, Ernest Hemmingway and Orson Welles spent summers here.

RIGHT:
Plaza de Toros, Ronda
With a diameter of 66m (217ft), this 18th-century bullring is the widest in Spain, although its stands have room for only a small crowd of 5000 spectators.

OPPOSITE:
Puente Nuevo, Ronda
Ronda is divided by the deep canyon of the Guadalevín River, which is spanned by three bridges. The newest, Puente Nuevo, was completed in 1793 after 34 years of construction.

BOTH PHOTOGRAPHS:
Arcos de la Frontera, Andalucía
One of Andalucía's *pueblos blancos* ('white villages'), named for their whitewashed traditional buildings, Arcos is on a sandstone ridge above the Guadalete River. Perched near the town's highest point is the Basílica de Santa María de la Asunción, built on the foundations of a mosque. Nearby is the Castillo de Arcos, an Umayyad fort also rebuilt after the Reconquista. Below Arcos, the river is crossed by the iron San Miguel Bridge, which was built in 1920 to replace a succession of wooden and then stone bridges destroyed by floods.

OPPOSITE AND LEFT:
Iglesia de Santa María la Coronada, Medina-Sidonia, Andalucía
Built on the site of a former mosque, this 16th-century Gothic-Mudéjar church houses an intricate gilded and polychrome wooden altarpiece. The carvings include 168 figures and are centred on the Coronation of the Virgin Mary.

ABOVE:
Medina-Sidonia
This *pueblo blanco* was settled by the Phoenicians, Romans and Visigoths before it was conquered by the Umayyad general Musa ibn Nusayr in 712 CE. In 1264, the stronghold was captured by Alfonso X of Castile in his lengthy battles with the Nasrid Emirate of Granada.

Setenil de las Bodegas, Andalucía
Situated along a narrow gorge of the Guadalporcún River, Setenil has many houses nestled into the cliffs, constructed by enlarging natural caves or overhangs and building a front wall. Setenil was once famed for its bodegas (vineyards), which were wiped out by grape phylloxera, an insect pest that spread to Spain from the Americas in the 1870s.

Plaza de España, Vejer de la Frontera, Andalucía
Ringed by date palms, this azulejo-tiled fountain – featuring four spouting ceramic frogs – was built in the 1940s. It graces the *pueblo blanco*'s main square, which offers views over fields of sunflowers and sugar beets towards the distant Mediterranean Sea.

ABOVE TOP AND BOTTOM:
Zahara de la Sierra, Andalucía
Today, this *pueblo blanco* lies beside the Zahara-El Gastor reservoir, created in 1992 by the damming of the Guadalete River. The town is backed by a crag from which the remains of a 13th-century Nasrid castle watch over the valley.

RIGHT:
Santa María de la Mesa, Zahara de la Sierra
In the centre of Zahara's old town is the church of Santa María de la Mesa. Built between 1742 and 1779, the strikingly painted building exhibits both Baroque curlicues and Neoclassical formalities.

ALL PHOTOGRAPHS:
Mezquita-Catedral de Córdoba, Córdoba, Andalucía

Córdoba's masterful and highly influential Great Mosque was commissioned in 785 CE by Abd al-Rahman I, founder of the Umayyad dynasty that ruled much of the Iberian Peninsula for nearly three centuries. The hypostyle prayer hall (pictured left) has innovative double-tiered arches, a lower tier of horseshoes and an upper of semicircles. The mihrab (pictured above top) was part of a 10th-century expansion. It is the earliest known mihrab that is an actual room rather than a wall niche. The heptagonal room is capped by a shell-shaped cupola coated in Byzantine-style mosaics. The mosque was converted to a cathedral in 1236 after Córdoba was taken by the Kingdom of Castile.

ABOVE:
Stucco plasterwork art at the Alhambra
The Alhambra citadel was begun in 1238 on the orders of Muhammad I, founder of the Nasrid dynasty and first ruler of the Emirate of Granada, the last Muslim state on the Iberian Peninsula. The complex's Nasrid palaces showcase elaborately carved 14th-century stucco work, featuring vegetal motifs, geometric patterns and Arabic inscriptions.

RIGHT:
Alhambra, Granada
Sited on the defendable Sabika Hill, in the foothills of the Sierra Nevada, the Nasrid Alhambra not only contained palaces but a mosque, houses, public baths and a tannery. When Granada was surrendered in 1492, the citadel became the court of Ferdinand and Isabella. Additional towers and a Renaissance palace were added over the next century.

LEFT:
Patio de la Sultana, Generalife, Granada
A short stroll from the Alhambra is the Generalife, the summer palace of the Nasrid emirs of Granada. The palace's name comes from the Arabic *jannat al-'arīf* ('Garden of the Architect'). The complex was begun in the late 13th or early 14th century, but the arcades overlooking the pretty Patio de la Sultana were added in 1584–86 during the reign of Philip II.

ABOVE:
Patio de la Acequia, Generalife
The Generalife palace is centred on the Patio de la Acequia. The word *acequia* comes from the Arabic *al-saqiya*, meaning 'water canal'. The garden is split by water and walkways into four flowerbeds, a style inspired by Persian Charbagh gardens, which are based on the four gardens of Paradise mentioned in the Quran. The arches of the courtyard's northern pavilion have finely carved stucco decoration.

Castillo de la Calahorra, La Calahorra, Andalucía
Its forbidding towers resembling four pepperpots, this Italian Renaissance-style castle was built between 1509 and 1512 by the 1st Marquis de Cenete after an inspiring trip to Italy. The castle has been used as a filming location, including for the 1974 film *Stardust* and the 2022 series *House of the Dragon*.

Playa de Mónsul, Andalucía
In the Cabo de Gata-Níjar Natural Park, this quiet beach has been spared from overdevelopment. It is known for its volcanic rock formations and dark sand. Thanks to being the sole place in mainland Europe with a hot desert climate, the park has only drought-adapted plants, including prickly pears, dwarf fan palms and agaves.

The Balearic Islands

The major Balearic Islands are Mallorca, Menorca, Ibiza and Formentera, while smaller islands in the archipelago include Cabrera, S'Espalmador and Es Vedrà. The islands were formed by the uplift of the Balearic Promontory, which rose above the western Mediterranean Sea around 150 million years ago. The Balearics were first inhabited around 2500–2300 BCE by the Bell Beaker people, who paddled from eastern Spain or southern France. The eastern Balearics, namely Menorca and Mallorca, have dozens of megalithic sites from the Bronze Age Talaiotic culture, which developed here from the end of the 2nd millennium BCE. By the 8th century BCE, the Balearics had been settled by the Phoenicians, a major Mediterranean trading power who left the greatest marks of their presence in clubber-friendly Ibiza Town. The name of the archipelago may come from the Phoenician "*balearides*", meaning lightly armed soldiers. Phoenician colonists are also credited with naming Ibiza, calling it Ibossim, meaning "dedicated to Bes". The Romans, who took control in 123–121 BCE, supplied the names of the other major islands: Mallorca (from Insula Maior, meaning "larger island"), Menorca (from Insula Minor, meaning "smaller island") and Formentera (from Frumentarium, meaning "granary"). The following centuries saw settlement and ambitious building projects, from impregnable castles to soaring cathedrals, by the Umayyads and Aragonese.

OPPOSITE:

Cap de Formentor, Mallorca
Cap de Formentor is Mallorca's northernmost point. Until 1922, the peninsula was owned by poet Miquel Costa i Llobera. In 1875, he wrote in Catalan the Romantic poem "Lo Pi de Formentor" (Pine of Formentor), in which he describes a tree on the peninsula battling "with the winds that attack the shore, like a giant warrior".

ALL PHOTOGRAPHS:
Alcúdia, Mallorca
The old town of Alcúdia has a 14th-century wall (pictured above), which today protects a network of narrow restaurant- and bar-lined pedestrian streets. The nearby Church of St Jaume (pictured above top) was built in the 13th century but overhauled in the 19th century in Neo-Gothic style.

LEFT AND ABOVE:
Bellver Castle, Palma de Mallorca, Mallorca
One of the few circular castles in Europe, Bellver was built from 1300 to 1311 for James II, King of Mallorca and Lord of Montpellier. Bellver was first the fortified palace of the kings of Mallorca, then served as a prison for several centuries. In 1932, the building became a museum.

Nus de Sa Corbata, Mallorca
This narrow road winds hair-raisingly between the island's highest peaks in the Serra de Tramuntana. The route takes cyclists and drivers over the mountain saddle of Coll de Cal Reis toward the pretty seaside village of Sa Calobra.

ABOVE LEFT AND ABOVE RIGHT:
Fornalutx, Mallorca
Most homes in the mountain village of Fornalutx have stone walls, red-tiled roofs and green-painted shutters. The village gardens and surrounding fields are planted with orange and lemon trees. A popular trail for hikers is the route from here to Sóller and back, which offers impressive mountain views along the way.

RIGHT AND OPPOSITE:
Port de Sóller, Mallorca
This fishing port and resort sits in a horseshoe-shaped bay, with lighthouses on each of its rocky headlands. On the northern headland (pictured right) is the 1945 Sa Creu Lighthouse, next to the decaying shell of its predecessor. Since 1913, a tram (pictured opposite) has linked Port de Sóller to the town of Sóller, 5 km (3 miles) inland.

ALL PHOTOGRAPHS:
Cala Fornells, Mallorca
The resort of Cala Fornells hugs the rocky shore to the west of busier Peguera. At the resort's quieter western end is its eponymous beach, part soft sand and part rock. The beach is renowned as one of Mallorca's finest due to its crystal-clear water, which is beloved by snorkellers.

ABOVE AND RIGHT:
Cap de Formentor, Mallorca
Mallorca attracts cyclists who want to experience the island's famously winding, precipitous climbs and *colls*. These include Sa Calobra, Puig Major, Coll de Sóller, Femenia and Sa Creu. In addition to these road rides, there are challenging gravel rides in the lowlands to the south of the Serra de Tramuntana range.

OPPOSITE:
Platja de Formentor, Mallorca
Backed by pine forest, which offers welcome shade in the summer, this Blue Flag beach has a 1,000-m (3,300-ft) strip of white sand. Just offshore, seagrass meadows are a nursery for dozens of species of young fish and crustaceans.

LEFT AND ABOVE:
La Seu, Palma de Mallorca, Mallora
At 44 m (144 ft) high, the Cathedral of Santa Maria of Palma (commonly known as La Seu) has one of the tallest naves of any Gothic cathedral. The building was commissioned by James I of Aragon in 1229, to stand on the site of Palma's main mosque. The work was not finished until 1601, then began again in 1851 following an earthquake. The cathedral's rose windows are up to 12 m (39 ft) across and contain as many as 1,236 pieces of glass.

Castell de Cabrera, Cabrera
The uninhabited island of Cabrera lies off the southwest coast of Mallorca. It is part of Spain's largest national park, the 908 sq km (351 sq mile) Cabrera Archipelago Maritime-Terrestrial, which is visited by sperm, fin, pilot and humpback whales. On the island's cliffs are the ruins of a 14th-century castle. More than 5,000 French prisoners-of-war died here during the Peninsular War (1807–14) after supply ships failed to arrive.

ABOVE LEFT AND ABOVE RIGHT:
Dalt Vila, Ibiza
Ibiza Town's old quarter, known as Dalt Vila, is crowned by the Catalan Gothic Catedral de la Verge de les Neus, which sports an unusual trapezoid belltower. Nearby is the necropolis of Puig des Molins, a cemetery founded toward the end of the 7th century BCE by the Phoenicians.

RIGHT:
Es Vedrà, Ibiza
Off the southwest coast of Ibiza, this uninhabited rocky islet is the subject of many myths. It was said to be home to sirens who tried to lure the hero Odysseus as he sailed past. A local folk tale has it that two brothers came to the island to collect rock samphire to cure their sick father. They were forced to battle the giant who lived in the islet's caves.

ABOVE:
Ciutadella de Menorca, Menorca
The port of Ciutadella was founded by the Carthaginians, who were the major trading and military power in the western Mediterranean from the 4th century BCE until the Roman defeat of Carthage in 146 BCE. The port's narrow, restaurant-lined harbour is a haven for yachts and fishing boats. Every few years, the harbour experiences a *rissaga*, a rare phenomenon known as a meteotsunami, caused by sudden changes in air pressure due to storms. The highest *rissaga* waves have reached 4 m (13 ft).

RIGHT:
Taula, Trepucó, Menorca
The remains of a Talaiotic town were excavated at Trepucó by archaeologist Margaret Murray in 1931. The Talaiotic culture, which took shape on Menorca and Mallorca at the end of the 2nd millennium BCE, is named for its talaiots: megalithic buildings that may have been meeting places, dwellings or defensive structures. Talaiots pre-date the taulas (pictured) that were built close to them between 500 and 300 BCE. Taulas, which probably had a religious purpose, consist of a vertical monolith capped with a horizontal stone.

Binibeca Vell, Menorca
Despite the "vell" (old) in its name, Binibeca was designed in the 1960s by the Catalan Functionalist architect Francisco Barba Corsini. As an alternative to typical tourist developments, the architect's intention was to echo the Menorcan vernacular building style while enhancing rather than blotting the natural features of the landscape.

S'Espalmador
The uninhabited, privately owned island of S'Espalmador is separated from Formentera by a sandbar, along which it is possible to wade at low tide. The island's pristine beaches are visited by yachtspeople, canoeists and snorkellers.

ALL PHOTOGRAPHS:

Es Trucadors, Formentera
Formentera's northernmost peninsula, Es Trucadors, is in Ses Salines de Eivissa and Formentera Natural Park, which protects habitats including seagrass beds, dunes, salt flats and juniper groves. Walkers may catch a glimpse of the Formenteran subspecies of Pityusic lizard, which is more brightly coloured than its relatives.

The Canary Islands

These islands started to form 70 million years ago over a hotspot in the African plate. The seven major islands, as well as several smaller islets, grew from the ocean floor as lava flow piled upon lava flow. The region is still volcanically active, with the last eruption having taken place in 2021. Measured from the seafloor at 7500m (24,600ft), Tenerife's Mt Teide is the world's third tallest volcano. From largest to smallest, the major islands are Tenerife, Fuerteventura, Gran Canaria, Lanzarote, La Palma, La Gomera and El Hierro. The easternmost island, Fuerteventura, is 97km (60 miles) off the coast of Morocco. This location gives the islands a hot desert or semi-arid climate, yet ocean winds and currents give inland regions of the western islands La Gomera, Tenerife and La Palma a more humid climate, allowing laurel forest to grow. It was from North Africa that the Guanches, the first inhabitants of the Canaries, sailed around 2000 years ago. After the Spanish Conquest in the 15th century, many Guanches were killed or enslaved, but some survived to make their mark on the islands' culture. The whistled language of La Gomera, still practised today, was invented by the Guanches to communicate across the island's valleys. The archipelago's name, however, comes from neither the Guanches nor the Spanish, but perhaps from Roman sailors, who called them Canariae Insulae ('Islands of the Dogs') due to the giant lizards or possibly seals that they mistook for giant dogs.

OPPOSITE:

Iglesia Matriz de El Salvador, Santa Cruz de la Palma, La Palma
This 16th-century church has a fine Renaissance portal and a belltower made from blocks of volcanic stone. Inside is a wood and ceramic ceiling of intricate geometric patterns in the Mudéjar style, a form of craftsmanship named for the Muslims who remained in Spain following the Reconquista.

ALL PHOTOGRAPHS:
Santa Cruz de la Palma, La Palma
La Palma's capital was founded in the late 15th century and soon became an important trading post on the routes between the Americas and Europe. Its old town has many colonial-style, wooden-balconied merchants' homes dating from this heyday. Sited on a lava flow from the nearby La Caldereta crater, the town made plentiful use of basalt in its cobbled streets. Like all the island's beaches, the town beach is volcanic black sand.

Cumbre Nueva, La Palma
The Cumbre Nueva scarp in central La Palma is often capped by clouds that cascade downhill due to the Foehn effect. This effect can be seen on the downwind side of a mountain range: cool, moist air forms clouds and rain on the windward side of the mountains, and then warmer, dry air flows down the downwind slope, blowing clouds with it.

Caldera de Taburiente National Park, La Palma
This national park is centred on the Caldera de Taburiente, formed by a crater collapse and erosion of the shield volcano that created the island. The caldera is 9km (5.6 miles) wide and 1500m (4920ft) deep. In spring, a small flowering plant known as *pico de graja* covers the park in a red carpet.

Salinas de Fuencaliente, La Palma
On the southernmost point of La Palma are salt evaporation ponds for the harvesting of table salt. Ocean water is piped into the shallow pools, allowing the water to evaporate in the sun, leaving the salt behind. The ponds are close to the retired 1903 and active 1985 Fuencaliente lighthouses.

LEFT:

Puerto Naos, La Palma
The resort of Puerto Naos boasts the longest beach in La Palma at 600m (1970ft). Its black basaltic sand is speckled with green olivine crystals. The resort offers paragliding and nighttime scuba expeditions, as well as tours of the surrounding banana plantations.

ABOVE TOP:

Cumbre Vieja, La Palma
In the southern half of La Palma is the active volcanic ridge known as Cumbre Vieja. It last erupted in 2021, forcing the evacuation of around 7000 people. The 6.2km (3.9 mile) lava flow destroyed 3000 buildings and formed a new peninsula on the island's west coast.

ABOVE BOTTOM:

Cascada de los Tilos, La Palma
In the northeastern corner of La Palma is Los Tilos forest, a UNESCO biosphere reserve for its precious ecosystem of laurel forest. The subtropical forest of broadleaved trees flourishes in this area of mild temperatures and high rainfall, where rivers and waterfalls abound.

La Geria, Lanzarote
In Lanzarote's La Geria wine region, cone-shaped hollows 2–3m (6.6–10ft) deep have been dug in the volcanic ash to harvest dew and the sparse rainfall. Additionally protected from sirocco winds by semicircular walls, vines planted in the hollows produce malvasía, listán and moscatel grapes, which become Lanzarote DO wines.

ABOVE:

Mar de las Calmas Marine Reserve, El Hierro
This reserve was created in 1996 to protect the extraordinarily biodiverse ocean around El Hierro. The seabed and underwater caves are home to orange tree corals, dead man's fingers corals and beds of deep-sea oysters. Cetacean visitors include Gervais's beaked whales and bottlenose dolphins.

RIGHT:

El Sabinar, El Hierro
Deformed by the powerful prevailing winds, the thicket of twisted Phoenician juniper trees of El Hierro's western cliffs have become a symbol of the island. They are reached along a dirt track around 3km (1.8 miles) north of the Ermita de Nuestra Señora de los Reyes, in an area populated only by a scattering of shepherds' huts.

LEFT:

Auditorio de Tenerife Adán Martín, Santa Cruz, Tenerife
Completed in 2003, this pioneering auditorium was designed by Spanish architect Santiago de Calatrava, known the world over for his sculptural bridges and gravity-defying buildings. The auditorium's unique cantilevered arch, known as the 'great arc', resembles a cresting wave.

OVERLEAF:

Jameos del Agua, Lanzarote
This partly submerged volcanic tube was formed by an eruption of La Corona volcano. Such hollow tubes are created when the outer layers of a lava flow solidify fast, allowing the lava inside to continue flowing until the tube empties. The Jameos del Agua is home to an endemic species of crab just 1cm (0.4in) long, white and blind.

Roque Cinchado, El Teide National Park, Tenerife
Eroded by the wind, weirdly sculpted blocks of volcanic rock stand in the shadow of Mt Teide. One of the blocks, known as Roque Cinchado, appeared on Spain's old 1000 peseta banknotes. Teide's summit is the highest point in Spain, at 3715m (12,188ft). It is an active stratovolcano but has not erupted since 1909.

Picture Credits

Alamy: 5 (Werner Lerooy), 6 (Marcos Veiga), 10 top (Ian Dagnall), 10 bottom (David R. Frazier Photolibrary Inc), 13 (Associated Press), 14 (Andrey Khrobostov), 15 (Paul Lindsay), 24 (Eduardo Blanco), 34/35 (Jorge Ciscar), 38/39 (Xavier Fores Joana Roncero), 50 bottom, 52 bottom & 53 bottom (Hemis), 53 top (Peter Eastland), 54 (Stefano Politi Markovina), 58 bottom (Miguel Angelo Silva), 60 bottom (villorejo), 68 (Angelo D'Amico), 73 (Stefano Politi Markovina), 76 bottom (M Ramírez), 78 (Patrick Shyu), 80 top (Ian Dagnall), 81 (agefotostock), 83 (Anamaria Mejia), 85 top (Ian Paterson), 86 bottom (mauritius images GmbH), 87 bottom (Sandra Foyt), 88 top (Peter Horree), 88 bottom (guy harrop), 89 (Luca Quadrio), 94 (dleiva), 95 bottom (M.Brodie), 96/97 (Finnbarr Webster), 100 (Martin Leber), 101 (Martin Leber), 101 bottom (agefotostock), 102 (dani codina), 103 top (Joan Gil), 103 bottom (Radharc Images), 104 (agefotostock), 105 top (Hemis), 106 (Stefano Politi Markovina), 111 top (Kevin George), 112 (Keren Su/China Span), 113 bottom (Kevin Foy), 117 top (Juan Carlos Giménez Bixquert), 119 (Oleksii Leonov), 120 (Jose Lucas), 121 top (Peter Adams Photography), 122 & 123 bottom (agefotostock), 125 (blickwinkel), 126 (Stefano Politi Markovina), 127 top (nagelestock.com), 127 bottom (Ken Welsh), 128/129 (Pascal Saez/VWPics), 131 (James Schwabel), 132/133 (eye35.pix), 136 (Perry van Munster), 140/141 (Zoonar GmbH), 142 (Zoonar GmbH), 143 (Ben Welsh Premium), 144 (Rolf Richardson), 145 bottom (Hemis), 146/147 (Old Town Tourist), 150 (George Munday), 151 (Peter Horree), 154 (Stefano Valeri), 156 (agsaz), 157 top (antonio ciero reina), 157 bottom (Jose Miguel Sanchez), 158/159 (Jacek Sopotnicki), 160/161 (Aleksandrs Tihonovs), 162 top (Tomka), 162 bottom (malbraman), 164 (Roman Belogorodov), 165 bottom (ErnestoGravelpond), 169 (Jose Lucas), 170/171 (Ashley Cooper pics), 178 (Werner Lerooy), 180/181 (Marcos Molina), 182 bottom (Joana Kruse), 183 (Ian Shaw), 184 (Hans Blossey), 185 top (ArtesiaWells), 187 (robertharding), 188 (Cultura Creative RF), 190/191 (Tolo Balaguer), 192 top (Alexander Nikiforov), 193 top (travelstock44), 200 bottom (Jaime Franch Travel Photo), 210/211 (Biosphoto), 212 (mauritius images GmbH), 216 (Jaime Franch Travel Photo)

Dreamstime: 16/17 top (Rechitan Sorin), 25 (Jose Julio Millan Gutierrez), 46 bottom (Marktucan), 55 top (Anibal Trejo), 55 bottom (Lukasz Janyst), 56/57 (Srubsan), 58/59 top (Robert Zehetmayer), 59 bottom (Carlos Soler Martinez), 60 top (Joaquin Ossorio Castillo), 61 (Dudlajzov), 62 (Jjfarq), 63 top (Jose Julio Millan Gutierrez), 63 bottom (Dudlajzov), 64 (Edmund Holt), 69 top (Dudlajzov), 69 bottom (Alvaro German Vilela), 70/71 & 72 both (H368k742), 74 & 75 top (Rudolf Ernst), 77 bottom (Dudlajzov), 80 bottom (Emotionart), 82 top (Lukas Bischoff), 82 bottom (Photoaliona), 84 top (Pcfoo3), 85 bottom (Wan Rosli Wan Othman), 86/87 (Arsty), 90/91 (Andrew Baumert), 92/93 (Alexsalcedo), 92 bottom (Balakate), 93 bottom (Alberto Zamorano), 95 top (Sjankauskas), 98/99 (Anibal Trejo), 105 bottom (Leonid Andronov), 107 (Pedro Antonio Salaverría Calahorra), 108/109 (Salvacubells), 110 (Denis Kelly), 111 bottom (Tanaonte), 114 (Marcos Castillo), 116 (David Shaun Dodds), 117 bottom (Jozef Sedmak), 123 top (David Sanchez Paniagua Carvajal), 124 (Szymon Bartosz), 130 (Jose Ramon Pizarro Garcia), 131 bottom (Lachris77), 134 (Carlos Pérez), 135 (Anton Sheiko), 137 (Steve Ford), 138 (Alvaro German Vilela), 139 (Jacek Sopotnicki), 148 top (Jose Miguel Garcia Ortega), 148 bottom (Ivo De), 149 (Place-to-be), 152 both (Dziewul), 153 (Sean Pavone), 155, 163 & 168 (Diego Grandi), 172/173 (Anetlanda), 174 (Andrei Bortnikau), 176 (Krajinar), 177 top (Igor Sychev), 177 bottom (Andrei Bortnikau), 179 (Ventura69), 182 top left (Val_th), 182 top right (Zbynek Pospisil), 185 bottom (Nataliya Schmidt), 186 top (Aleh Varanishcha), 186 bottom (Peter Ková⊠), 189 (Saaaaaa), 194 (Dorinmarius), 198/199 (Alexandre Rosa), 200/201 (Ignasi Such), 202 (Rosshelen), 204 (Aguaviva), 205 top (Dudlajzov), 218/219 (Tommycahill), 220/221 (Meinzahn), 222 (Peter Zaharov), 223 (Mistervlad)

Getty Images: 20 (Cesar Manso), 65 top (Domingo Leiva), 65 bottom (Jonatan Martin), 75 bottom (Manuel Romaris), 76 top (Sergio Formoso), 77 top (Sir Francis Canker Photography), 84 bottom (Alexander Spatari), 113 top (Gonzalo Azumendi), 115 (Gonzalo Azumendi), 201 bottom (Guido Cozzi/Atlantide Phototravel), 205 bottom, 206/207 & 208/209 (Dominic Dähncke), 213 top (Antonio Luis Martinez Cano), 213 bottom (perlaroques)

Shutterstock: 7 (Fernando Garcia Esteban), 8 (Arthur C.C. Hsieh), 11 (Kaos Photo), 12 (Jarno Gonzalez Zarraonandia), 16 bottom left (Jesus De Fuensanta), 16 bottom right (Jakub Korczyk), 18 top (Icruci), 18 bottom (acongar), 19 (Irma Sanchez), 21 top & bottom (barmalini), 22/23 (David Herraez Calzada), 26 (Marques), 27 (Joaquin Ossorio Castillo), 28/29 (Iryna Horbachova), 30/31 (FCG), 32 (roberaten), 33 (Dmi.Bo.S), 36/37 (imagestockdesign), 40/41 (Miguel Moya Moreno), 42/43 (Francesco Bonino), 44/45 (Gonzalo Buzonni), 46 top (Yuri Dondish), 47 (Biloba World), 48 (Songquan Deng), 50 top (R.M. Nunes), 51 (Sergii Figurnyi), 52 top (Omri Eliyahu), 66/67 Sean Pavone, 121 bottom (barmalini), 145 top Sean Pavone, 166 (joserpizarro), 167 (Macronatura.es), 192/193 (Charles Brongniart), 195 (tolobalaguer.com), 196/197 (Kite_rin), 214/215 (F. Jimenez Meca), 217 (David Herraez Calzada)